LANGUAGE ARTS EXPLORER

THE
U.S. CIVIL WAR
AND
RECONSTRUCTION

1850 to 1877

by Brian Howell

HISTORY DIGS

CHERRY LAKE PUBLISHING · ANN ARBOR, MICHIGAN

CHERRY LAKE
Publishing

Published in the United States of America
by Cherry Lake Publishing
Ann Arbor, Michigan
www.cherrylakepublishing.com

Printed in the United States of America
Corporate Graphics Inc
September 2011
CLFA09

Consultants: Brett Barker, associate professor of history, University of Wisconsin–
Marathon County; Gail Saunders-Smith, associate professor of literacy, Beeghly College of
Education, Youngstown State University

Editorial direction: Design and production:
Rebecca Rowell   Marie Tupy

Photo credits: Library of Congress, cover, 1, 8, 14, 17, 23; Alexander Gardner/Library of
Congress, 5, 18; North Wind Picture Archives, 7, 13; W. H. Rease/Library of Congress, 10; Nic
Taylor/iStockphoto, 15; William Sherman/iStockphoto, 20; W. Roberts/R.A. Dimmick/Library of
Congress, 25, 30; Shutterstock Images, 27

Library of Congress Cataloging-in-Publication Data
Howell, Brian, 1974-
 The US Civil War and Reconstruction / by Brian Howell.
    p. cm. – (Language Arts Explorer : History digs.)
 ISBN 978-1-61080-201-7 – ISBN 978-1-61080-289-5 (pbk.)
 1. United States–History–Civil War, 1861-1865–Juvenile literature. 2. Reconstruction (U.S.
history, 1865-1877)–Juvenile literature. I. Title.
 E468H88 2011
 973.8–dc22

                            2011015126

**Cherry Lake Publishing would like to acknowledge the work of The Partnership for
21st Century Skills. Please visit www.21stCenturySkills.org for more information.**

TABLE OF CONTENTS

You are being given a mission. The facts in What You Know will help you accomplish it. Remember the clues from What You Know while you are reading the story. The clues and the story will help you answer the questions at the end of the book. Have fun on this adventure!

YOUR MISSION

Your mission is to learn to think like a historian. What tools do historians use to research the past? What kinds of questions do they ask, and where do they look for answers? On this assignment, your goal is to learn about the Civil War. What were the causes of the war? What role did Abraham Lincoln play in the war? How did the war affect the United States? How did the United States rebuild after the war? As you read, keep the facts in What You Know in mind.

WHAT YOU KNOW

★ Before the Civil War, part of the United States practiced slavery and part did not.

★ The South **seceded** from the Union.

★ During the Civil War, Lincoln came to support the abolition of slavery.

★ The North, which was against slavery, beat the South to win the Civil War.

★ Slavery was **abolished** as a result of the Civil War.

Use this book to explore history in ways a historian might. Read the following journal to discover what one student learned about this time period while helping launch a new Civil War museum in town.

Lincoln had the challenging task
of trying to lead a country that was divided.

My teacher said the new building near school is a museum about the Civil War. That got me very excited. The Civil War was one of my favorite topics in history class. Last week, I stopped by the museum and saw workers moving items inside. I met a woman, Isabel Lucas, who told me they were setting up all of the **exhibits** in the museum. She is a **curator** at the museum. I asked her if I could work as a volunteer to help set up the exhibits. Luckily, she said yes, so I'm spending the week of spring break working at the museum.

Firsthand Accounts

Today was my first day at the museum. I helped Isabel set up an exhibit about slavery. I saw many **artifacts**, including tools slaves used to farm and chains traders and owners used to keep the enslaved captive. There was also the story of a man named Olaudah Equiano. He was an African who had been captured as a boy and sold into slavery. As an adult, he wrote his **autobiography**. He described his journey on the ship that took him from his homeland:

> The closeness of the place, and the heat of the climate, added to the number in the ship, which was so crowded that each had scarcely room to turn himself, almost suffocated us. . . . The air soon became unfit for respiration . . . and brought on a sickness among the slaves, of which many died. . . . The shrieks of the women, and the groans of the dying, rendered the whole a scene of horror almost inconceivable.

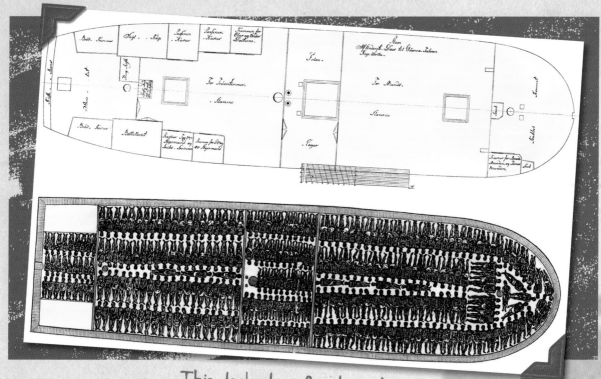

This deck plan of a slave ship shows how captured Africans were arranged as cargo.

The display included audio. I unpacked the headsets visitors will use to listen to recordings of real former slaves talking about their experiences. Isabel said these firsthand accounts are important historical resources. They allow listeners to understand what slavery was like for those who were enslaved in the 1800s.

I listened to one of the recordings. It was an interview with a man named Fountain Hughes. He had been born a slave in Virginia in 1848. He was interviewed in 1949, when he was 101 years old. Hughes explained that his grandfather had been owned by Thomas Jefferson. He talked about being born a slave and working as one: "Time to cut tobacco. If they want you to cut all night long out in the field, you cut. And if they want you to hang all night long, you hang—

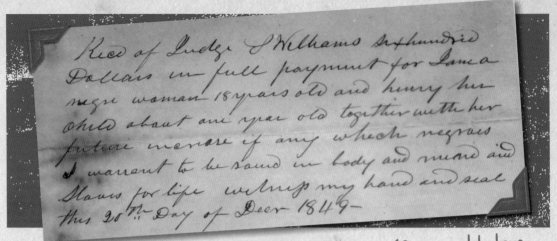

This is a receipt for the purchase of Jane, an 18-year-old slave, her one-year-old child, Henry, and any future children. The receipt is dated December 20, 1849.

hang tobacco. It didn't matter about you're tired. Being tired, you're afraid to say you're tired."

The museum had several of these recordings. I learned a lot from them and other artifacts in the display. I was curious to know how slavery led to the Civil War. Isabel said I'd find out this week. ★

PRIMARY SOURCES

Olaudah Equiano's autobiography, in which he described his voyage from Africa in a slave ship, is a primary source. So are documents created by Abraham Lincoln, such as speeches and letters. Primary sources come directly from the people or era being studied. Photographs are another type of primary source. In recent decades, e-mail has become a primary source. All of these artifacts help historians understand the people who created them and the period in which they were created.

I helped Isabel with a display about Abraham Lincoln today. As president of the United States, he was an important figure during the Civil War. I unpacked copies of law books Lincoln used and a replica of his famous stovepipe hat. Other artifacts included copies of photographs and documents from before Lincoln became president and from during his presidency.

Isabel explained that since Lincoln lived before television and radio were invented, we have to rely mostly on handwritten and printed materials such as speeches, letters, and newspapers for historical information about him.

In His Own Words

The first document I saw was a speech. Isabel said it is known as the "House Divided" speech. She explained that Lincoln gave it in his home state of Illinois in 1858 when he was launching his campaign to become a U.S. senator. Some of the words caught my attention:

> "A house divided against itself cannot stand." I believe this government cannot endure permanently half slave and half free. I do not expect the Union to be dissolved; I do not expect the house to fall; but I do expect it will cease to be divided. It will become all one thing, or all the other.

I asked Isabel what house Lincoln was talking about. She reminded me of our discussion yesterday about slavery. She said

This campaign banner for the 1860 presidential election shows one way candidates ran for office during that period.

the house was the United States and that Lincoln was predicting the nation would eventually become all slave states or all free states.

First Inaugural Address

I picked up another document. Only two years later, in 1860, Lincoln was elected president of the United States. When he was sworn into office in 1861, Lincoln gave his first **inaugural** address— I learned in history class that he would give a second address because he was reelected in 1864. I looked at the words he had written. In that speech, he pleaded with Americans to come together. He wanted the country to avoid a civil war. He said:

In your hands, my dissatisfied fellow countrymen, and not in mine, is the momentous issue of civil war. . . . We are not enemies, but friends. We must not be enemies. Though passion may have strained it must not break our bonds of affection.

Reading Lincoln's speeches was exciting. I could tell that Lincoln felt strongly about keeping the United States together. I told Isabel I thought Lincoln was a great speaker. She said a lot of people then did, too, and that is why he was elected president. She also noted that he wasn't popular with everyone and that his passion wasn't enough to keep the country united. She said I'd learn more about that tomorrow. ★

PRESIDENTIAL LIBRARIES AND MUSEUMS

There are 13 official presidential libraries managed by the federal government. They are not typical libraries. They are archives and museums, housing information specific to a particular president, his life, and his time in office. The presidential library system began in 1939 when Franklin D. Roosevelt donated his papers to the federal government. In 1955, the Presidential Libraries Act created the system that exists today. There are presidential libraries outside this system, including the Abraham Lincoln Presidential Library and Museum in Springfield, Illinois. It has many Lincoln artifacts. It is maintained by the Illinois Historic Preservation Agency.

Today, we set up artifacts and information about the Confederacy. I knew about the Confederate flag and that Southern states separated from the rest of the nation, but I didn't know much more than that. As I unpacked materials for the display, I asked Isabel to tell me why the South seceded.

The Issue of Expansion

Isabel explained that the 1800s was a time of expansion in the United States. The Louisiana Purchase in 1803 more than doubled the size of the nation. And territory in the West, such as California, was added following the Mexican-American War, which was fought from 1846 to 1848.

I continued to unpack items as Isabel talked. I found different maps of the United States. No two were the same. They showed how the nation grew in size. I also found several documents. They weren't like the handwritten letters in the Lincoln exhibit. They seemed more official. The documents had different numbers, such as 1820, 1850, and 1854. I asked Isabel about them. She said they were copies of laws enacted in the 1800s. The laws led to the Civil War.

I wondered how laws could lead to war. Isabel said the laws addressed the expansion of slavery into new U.S. territories. Some people wanted slavery to be an option in the new states, but others didn't. Isabel told me more about the laws.

In 1820, the U.S. Congress passed the Missouri Compromise. It was the idea of Henry Clay, a senator from Kentucky. It created a balance between slave and free states. It allowed Missouri to enter the Union as a slave state and Maine to enter as a free state. It also

Maps such as this one of the Compromise of 1850 are helpful because they present information with images.

banned slavery in the remainder of the land from the Louisiana Purchase located north of Missouri's southern border. The plan worked for 25 years.

Next, Isabel told me about the Compromise of 1850. Clay worked on this compromise too. It was a series of laws to satisfy the people who supported slavery and those who did not. It included admitting California as a free state and giving the South the Fugitive Slave Law. Both sides were upset by what the other side got and neither side was pleased.

Compromise Resolutions—Mr. Clay.

...ation in the
...g them in the
...The poorest
...it, and seal
...blood which
...ction in the
...als; they are
...riors. They
...continue so.
...be overcome
...up in their
...war between
...rmination to
...hich history
...fanaticism,
...ld press it to
...the North,
...g hand. Is
...no grievance
...complain of
...rily bringing

...ustice, I de-
...ed by north-
...f the Union,
...and won by
...lized by the
...no part nor
...to be formed
...dmitted into
...equals? I
...s freemen—
...Our fathers
...eir sons are
...ty, but with
...rts and firm
...outh cannot
...riority to be

...Are you
...e, there will
...d happiness.
...as intended
...eak—should
...outh and the
...North ap-
...box has be-
...nd ask us to
...charter; we
...n which our
...principles of
...d them will
...gentlemen,
...ask but our
...to the wall,
...k will meet
...But your
...oly crusade.
...r our wives,

weakest member of the North should be felt by every southern heart—and a wound inflicted upon the feeblest southern State should meet with a generous response in every northern bosom. An injury by a stranger's hand is felt and resented—but oh! how painful the wound and bitter the feelings when inflicted by a brother's. I beseech you to pause—by the memories of the past and the hopes of the future—break not the last golden cord—let us weave them anew and bind them around the Union with the patriotic fervor of our noble ancestors. Let us come together with brotherly love, and sacrifice upon the altar of the Union, every unhappy sectional feeling; let the pure incense of patriotism ascend from *our hearts*, which did from those of Washington, of Hancock, of Madison, of Adams. Let us think of the glorious destiny before us, with a *"perfect Union;"* let us think of the millions who are to succeed us, and the curses which will rest upon us, should we be faithless to the sacred trust we hold for posterity—think of the oppressed nations of the earth who are looking with hope to our beacon light of freedom. Oh, extinguish not that light! Crush not those hopes! Let that "mustard seed" which our fathers planted, grow until its roots shall penetrate earth's centre, and its branches spread until all nations shall rest in peace and liberty under its shade. Brethren of the North, let your patriotism rise with the crisis—the times require it—not a moment can be lost; think not of "political tombstones"—think of our country—take the responsibility of saving the Union. It is in your hands. Tell your constituents so. The upheaving of the national bosom will sustain you. It requires stout hearts and firm nerves. You have both. Do it! Posterity will rise up and call you blessed. "The Union *one* and indivisible, now and forever"—but *the Union with the Constitution.*

COMPROMISE RESOLUTIONS.

SPEECH OF MR. CLAY,

OF KENTUCKY,

In the Senate of the United States,

February 5 and 6, 1850,

In support of his Resolutions proposing an amicable arrangement of all questions in controversy between the Free and the Slave States, growing out of the subject of Slavery.

The Senate proceeded to the consideration of the following Resolutions, submitted by Mr. CLAY on the 29th ultimo:

It being desirable, for the peace, concord, and harmony of the Union of these States, to settle and adjust amicably all existing questions of controversy between them, arising out of the institution of slavery, upon a fair, equitable, and just basis: Therefore,

1st. *Resolved,* That California, with suitable boundaries,

6th. *But Resolved,* That it is expedier the District the slave-trade, in slaves b States or places beyond the limits of the sold therein as merchandise, or to be t markets without the District of Columb

7th. *Resolved,* That more effectual pr made by law, according to the requireme tion, for the restitution and delivery of p vice or labor in any State, who may esc State or Territory in the Union.

And 8th. *Resolved,* That Congress ha hibit or obstruct the trade in slaves betw ing States; but that the admission or brought from one into another of them, upon their own particular laws.

Mr. CLAY addressed the Senat

Mr. PRESIDENT, never, on any have I risen under feelings of such I have witnessed many periods o of peril, and of danger even to th have never before arisen to addre so oppressed, so appalled, so anx I hope it will not be out of place again and again I have done in m ber—to implore of Him who hol of nations and individuals in his upon our country his blessings— our people all his blessings—to c and rage of party—to still passio son once more to resume its empi not ask of Him, to bestow upon vant, now before Him, the blessin of strength, and of ability, to pe which lies before him.

Sir, I have said that I have anxious periods in the history of if I were to mention—to trace t source—the cause of all our pres difficulties, I should ascribe them and intemperance of party spirit. testimony of this in the progress and Senators, however they may matters, concur in acknowledgin of that cause in originating the unh which prevail throughout the co subject of the institution of slave their endeavors to obtain the one over the other, catch at every pass plank, in order to add strength and selves. We have been told by Senators, [Mr. HALE and Mr. P parties at the North have each in and endeavored to obtain the small party called Abolitionists, in scale in its favor might preponde versaries. Let us look wherever too many indications of the existe and intemperance of party. I m legislative bodies besides our ow from those Legislatures all the upon which I am dwelling; b pass out of this Capitol

Government documents are valuable resources for understanding history.
This one shows Clay's speech to the U.S. Senate
in support of the resolutions of the Compromise of 1850.

I asked Isabel about the law passed in 1854. She said the Kansas-Nebraska Act renewed the conflict over slavery in the western United States. It **repealed** the prohibition of slavery established by the Missouri Compromise. It was clear that slavery was a **divisive** issue. People just couldn't agree on it. I remembered Lincoln's "House Divided" speech and understood why he gave it.

Lincoln the Republican

Isabel went on to explain that although Lincoln wanted to keep the states united, his election actually led to their separation. I was surprised. He was so **passionate** about the nation remaining **intact**. Isabel said that during the conflict over the expansion of slavery in the 1850s, a new political party formed in the North known as the Republican Party. Republicans opposed the spread of slavery to new territories. Southern politicians, thinking slavery must expand or die, were concerned about the Republican Party. Isabel said they feared that Republicans might want to abolish slavery in the South.

While people in the North and the South believed that states had many powers, most Southerners believed their states' rights included the right to secede from the Union. Many northerners argued that their states were powerful, but the Union of the states was permanent and could not be broken up. And when Lincoln was elected the first Republican president in November 1860, several slave states made a dramatic decision.

Isabel said seven states seceded and formed the Confederate States of America. It was hard for me to imagine. As Isabel and I

THE CONFEDERACY

Eventually, 11 states seceded from the Union. Following a meeting on December 20, 1860, South Carolina separated first. In January, Mississippi, Florida, Alabama, Georgia, and Louisiana decided to secede. Texas made the decision on February 1, 1861. The remaining four states, the Upper South, seceded after the battle at Fort Sumter, South Carolina. They were Arkansas, North Carolina, Tennessee, and Virginia.

talked, I went back to the maps for the display. One showed the states divided. I clearly saw the division between the North and the South. Isabel told me the Confederacy had its own president—Jefferson Davis—its own constitution, and its own flag. I found a replica of both among the artifacts.

When Lincoln was inaugurated as the sixteenth U.S. president, he had to deal with the Confederacy. I thought it was probably a difficult job. Isabel said it was and that a month after Lincoln was sworn in as president, the situation got worse. U.S. troops had long been stationed at forts in Charleston, South Carolina. South Carolina, which had seceded, demanded that Lincoln abandon Fort Sumter, but he refused. I was eager to know more. Isabel said we would discuss it more when we set up the war display. The afternoon had gone so quickly, and I had learned so much. I can't wait to come back and help more. ★

I got to the museum a little early today. I was eager to see the artifacts the museum had about the Civil War. This was the display Isabel said we'd set up this afternoon. I knew the war started at Fort Sumter. Isabel told me that the number of states in the Confederacy grew from seven to 11 after that battle when the states in the Upper South seceded.

Learning from the Numbers

Just like the Confederacy display, the war display had maps. But I unpacked a lot more today than I did yesterday. Each map was

This record from October 3, 1862, provides details of the Union's Ninth Army Corps at Antietam.

This photograph shows Lincoln meeting with some of his troops at Antietam, Maryland.

labeled with the name of a battle. There were so many, such as Shiloh, Antietam, Fredericksburg, and Gettysburg. Each map included information about the battle. One map showed the Battle of Shiloh. It began April 6, 1862. In two days of fighting, there were more than 20,000 casualties: 13,047 Union and 10,699 Confederate. Isabel said it was an early and bloody battle of the war. I learned something interesting. The name *Shiloh* came from the name of a church near the fighting. It is a Hebrew word that means "place of peace."

I looked at another map. The Battle of Antietam took place on September 17, 1862. It also had more than 20,000 casualties: 12,401 Union and 10,318 Confederate. This battle was fought in one day.

Isabel said it was the worst single day of battle during the entire war and the deadliest day in U.S. history.

As I studied more maps, I got a better idea of the war. I saw where the fighting occurred and how many soldiers died. I was amazed. There were so many casualties. Isabel said more than 2 million men fought and almost 620,000 died.

The Gettysburg Address

When I got to the map of the Battle of Gettysburg, I remembered one of Lincoln's speeches. I could see from the statistics that the battle fought in early July 1863 was the worst battle of the war. Both sides suffered terrible losses.

I understood why the battle site in Pennsylvania was made into a national cemetery. Lincoln gave his Gettysburg Address at the dedication ceremony. He began with these now-famous words: "Four score and seven years ago our fathers brought forth on this continent a new nation, conceived in liberty and dedicated to the proposition that all men are created equal."

I thought about the idea of people being created equal and how not everyone believed that since slavery existed.

The Emancipation Proclamation

After setting up the maps, I organized photographs. I found some with black soldiers. I asked Isabel about them. She explained that African Americans fought for the North. At the beginning of the war, Lincoln struggled for military success. He also faced Northerners calling for an end to slavery. These led him to emancipate, or free, the slaves in the South.

On January 1, 1863, Lincoln issued the Emancipation Proclamation. Isabel said it made a big difference in the war. It did not abolish slavery everywhere right away, but it made freeing slaves in the South a goal for the North. It also allowed Lincoln's army to recruit blacks. Isabel said almost 200,000 African Americans fought for the North as part of the army and navy.

The War Ends

It was almost time to go for the day. As I finished helping Isabel with the display, we talked about the war coming to an end. After four years of fighting and so much loss, the war ended when the South surrendered to the North on April 9, 1865. I asked Isabel what happened next in the South. She said we'd talk about that tomorrow while setting up the Reconstruction display. ★

WATER WAR

The Civil War was fought on land and in water. The battle between the North's *Monitor* and the South's *Virginia* was the first time two ironclad ships had ever fought. Their battle on March 9, 1862, ended in a stalemate. The war had another historic battle at sea. On February 17, 1864, the South's *H. L. Hunley* sank the North's *Housatonic*. It was the first time a submarine sank its target.

Today was my last day volunteering at the museum. I worked on a display about the years following the war. It was an era called Reconstruction. I thought the era was about rebuilding the things that had been destroyed during the war, such as houses and farms. However, Isabel told me Reconstruction was much more than that. It was more about **restructuring** the South politically.

Presidential Plans

As Isabel and I talked, I sorted through artifacts. I found several documents. They had different labels, such as *proclamation*, *amendment*, and *code*. Isabel began telling me about some proclamations from the time. Plans for reconstructing the South began during the war. In 1863, Lincoln issued the Proclamation of Amnesty and Reconstruction. It said he would recognize any state that would declare loyalty to the Union and the U.S. Constitution and free its slaves. All that was needed was support by 10 percent of the number of people who voted in the 1860 presidential election. Isabel said state governments loyal to the Union were created in Arkansas, Louisiana, and Tennessee following this plan.

I learned that Andrew Johnson was a Democrat before the war, a member of the other major political party. He was also from the South. He helped reorganize the loyal government in Tennessee, and his success led to becoming vice president when Lincoln was reelected in 1864. But Johnson wasn't vice president for very long.

When Lincoln was assassinated on April 15, 1865, as the war was coming to an end, Johnson became president. He had his own plan for Reconstruction. To rejoin the Union, a state had to write a constitution, pledge loyalty to the U.S. Constitution, repeal their declarations of secession, have its loyal citizens create a government, and accept the Thirteenth Amendment—the change to the Constitution that abolished slavery.

I asked Isabel if the Southern states were punished for seceding. She said they were not and explained that Johnson issued a proclamation pardoning them. She also said the federal government did not provide much guidance during this period. Initially, some **oversight** was given, but that lessened over the years. I was surprised to learn that states in the South could pretty much do what they wanted.

That's when Isabel told me about the codes I found. Many of these states adopted black codes to control African Americans by limiting their rights. For example, Mississippi made it unlawful for blacks and whites to marry. Other black codes limited African Americans' ability to own land. Southern states accepted abolition, but they were reluctant to accept African Americans as equal.

Fourteenth and Fifteenth Amendments

Next, Isabel told me about the amendments passed during Reconstruction. I had learned in history class that the Thirteenth Amendment had been **ratified** in late 1865 and ended slavery in the United States. I did not know about the other amendments in the display.

Not everyone liked Johnson's plan. Isabel said the U.S. Congress ended Johnson's Reconstruction program for fear that it would leave African Americans in a position similar to slavery, with few rights. Many Northern politicians also worried that Southerners who held power during secession would regain power.

Andrew Johnson helped rebuild the country after the Civil War.

Isabel explained that from 1866 to 1869, Congress created new laws and amendments to give African Americans more rights. I studied the two amendments to find out what they meant.

The Fourteenth Amendment was passed by Congress in 1866. It was ratified in 1868. It granted African Americans citizenship. It also gave them civil and legal rights:

> No state shall make or enforce any law which shall abridge the privileges or immunities of citizens of the United States; nor shall any state deprive any person of life, liberty, or property, without due process of law; nor deny to any person within its jurisdiction the equal protection of the laws.

The Fifteenth Amendment was passed by Congress in 1869 and was ratified in 1870. It gave all male citizens the right to vote, including African American men. I was surprised by the shortness of the amendment. One sentence granted the right to vote, and another stated that Congress has the right to enforce that right. Such a **monumental** change was made in so few words.

Redemption

Isabel explained that the changes were significant on paper, but that it took a long time for them to become reality. I didn't understand what she meant. She said Democrats in the South used fear and violence to win elections there. Then, they used their positions to gradually take away African Americans' political and economic gains.

By the time Reconstruction ended in 1877, all Southern states were something called "redeemed." Isabel said it meant that Southern Democrats regained power and stood up to the North. The South had returned to a way of life as close as it could get to slavery. African Americans had few rights as a result of laws created by Southern Democrats. Although African Americans were free, they lived in a society that left them disadvantaged socially and politically.

I remembered learning about segregation in school and mentioned it to Isabel. She said I could come back and visit her anytime to discuss that and the Civil War. I thanked her for helping me learn so much about the war, Reconstruction, and the importance of artifacts in understanding history. I told her I'd be back soon to learn more. ★

THE RIGHT TO VOTE

In 1870, the Fifteenth Amendment granted all American men the right to vote. However, many African American men experienced it more as a promise, not reality. Southern states created laws that kept African American men from voting. These included poll taxes, which many could not afford, and literacy tests, which many could not pass. It would take almost 100 years before many blacks in the South could vote. The Voting Rights Act of 1965 finally made it illegal to hinder a person's right to vote.

MISSION ACCOMPLISHED!

You did it! You learned about the Civil War and Reconstruction. You learned that slavery was the main cause of the division between the North and the South, which led to the Civil War. You read about how Abraham Lincoln was an influential speaker who guided the country through the Civil War. You examined how the war caused destruction and casualties. You learned that Reconstruction was much more than rebuilding homes and farms. Nice work!

CONSIDER THIS

★ What do you think of Southern states seceding? Would that be possible today?

★ If you had been president instead of Lincoln, how might you have dealt with secession and the war? What would you have done differently than Lincoln?

★ What do you think it was like for Americans during the Civil War to have their nation so divided?

★ Southern Democrats fought to keep African Americans from being equal to them. Why do you think that is?

IN THIS TEMPLE
AS IN THE HEARTS OF THE PEOPLE
FOR WHOM HE SAVED THE UNION
THE MEMORY OF ABRAHAM LINCOLN
IS ENSHRINED FOREVER

The Lincoln Memorial was built in honor of the president.
You can visit the site in Washington, DC.

GLOSSARY

abolish (uh-BAH-lish) to get rid of something completely

artifact (AHR-tuh-fakt) an object made by people in the past

autobiography (aw-toh-bye-AH-gruh-fee) a book a person writes about his or her life

curator (KYOO-ray-tur) the person who chooses and organizes the items in museum displays

divisive (di-VYE-siv) causing disagreement and separation into groups

exhibit (ig-ZIB-it) a collection of objects placed in a public area for people to see

inaugural (in-AW-gyuhr-uhl) happening as part of an official ceremony when someone starts an important job, such as president

intact (in-TAKT) complete, together

monumental (mahn-yuh-MEN-tuhl) very important

oversight (OH-vur-site) the act of directing or guiding work

passionate (PASH-uh-nit) to have or show strong feelings

ratify (RAT-uh-fye) to pass or approve

repeal (ri-PEEL) to officially cancel a law

resolution (rez-uh-LOO-shun) a formal announcement or statement of an opinion or decision by a group, such as the U.S. Senate

secede (si-SEED) to officially break away from a group

stalemate (STALE-mate) a situation when no one clearly wins

LEARN MORE

BOOKS

Hamilton, Virginia. *Many Thousand Gone: African Americans from Slavery to Freedom.* New York, NY: Knopf, 2002.

King, David C. *Civil War and Reconstruction.* Hoboken, NJ: Wiley, 2003.

Marrin, Albert. *Commander in Chief: Abraham Lincoln and the Civil War.* New York, NY: Dutton Children's Books, 2003.

Pascal, Janet. *Who Was Abraham Lincoln?* New York, NY: Grosset & Dunlap, 2008.

Stanchack, John. *Civil War.* New York, NY: Dorling Kindersley, 2000.

WEB SITES

Civil War 150
http://www.civilwar150.si.edu/

It has been more than 150 years since the Civil War began. This Smithsonian Institution site commemorates the anniversary with information and links to helpful resources.

The Time of the Lincolns
http://www.pbs.org/wgbh/amex/lincolns/

Explore this PBS site to learn what life was like when Abraham Lincoln and his wife lived.

FURTHER MISSIONS

MISSION 1

As president, Abraham Lincoln was a powerful leader who influenced many people. Find out more about the presidency and what the office entails. Explore how the current president has influenced the United States and the world.

MISSION 2

From the mid-1600s to 1865, most black people in the United States were slaves. They were treated as inferior and had no rights. Today, some of the most powerful and famous men and women in the country are African American. Find out more about the most influential African Americans of today. Write about one man and one woman. Explain who they are. Why are they famous? What makes them powerful? What are their backgrounds? What do you admire about them?

Lincoln took advantage of his position to issue the Emancipation Proclamation.

INDEX

ABOUT THE AUTHOR

Brian Howell is a freelance writer. He has a bachelor's degree in journalism with a minor in history. He writes about sports and history. He lives with his wife and four children in his native Colorado.

ABOUT THE CONSULTANTS

Brett Barker is an associate professor of history at the University of Wisconsin-Marathon County in Wausau. He received his PhD in history from the University of Wisconsin-Madison and his MA and BA in history from Ohio State University. He has worked with K-12 teachers in two Teaching American History grants.

Gail Saunders-Smith is a former classroom teacher and Reading Recovery teacher leader. Currently, she teaches literacy courses at Youngstown State University in Ohio. Gail is the author of many books for children and three professional books for teachers.